WHY ARE ANIMALS ENDANGERED?

BY ISAAC ASIMOV

Gareth Stevens Publishing
MILWAUKEE

For a free color catalog describing Gareth Stevens' list of high-quality books, call
1-800-542-2595 (USA) or 1-800-461-9120 (Canada). Gareth Stevens' Fax: (414) 225-0377.

Library of Congress Cataloging-in-Publication Data

Asimov, Isaac
     Why are animals endangered? / by Isaac Asimov.
          p.   cm. — (Ask Isaac Asimov)
     Includes bibliographical references and index.
     Summary: Discusses why certain animals have become endangered
and what can be done to help them from becoming extinct.
     ISBN 0-8368-0798-7
     1. Endangered species--Juvenile literature. 2. Wildlife conservation--
Juvenile literature. [1. Rare animals. 2. Wildlife conservation.]
     I. Title. II. Series: Asimov, Isaac. Ask Isaac Asimov.
     QL83.A75   1992
     591.52'9--dc20   92-5346

Edited, designed, and produced by
Gareth Stevens Publishing
1555 North RiverCenter Drive, Suite 201
Milwaukee, Wisconsin 53212, USA

Text © 1992 by Nightfall, Inc. and Martin H. Greenberg
End matter © 1992 by Gareth Stevens, Inc.
Format © 1992 by Gareth Stevens, Inc.

Picture Credits
pp. 2-3, © John Cancalosi/Bruce Coleman Limited; pp. 4-5, © Peter Davey/Bruce Coleman Limited; pp. 6-7, Michael
Medynsky/Artisan, 1992; pp. 8-9, Durant Ball, 1992; pp. 10-11, © Udo Hirsch/Bruce Coleman Limited; pp. 12-13, ©
Martin Wendler/NHPA; pp. 14-15, © Gordon Langsbury/Bruce Coleman Limited; p. 15 (inset), © Wayne
Lankinen/Bruce Coleman Limited; pp. 16-17, © Herbert Girardet/Still Pictures; p. 16 (insets), Durant Ball, 1992; pp.
18-19, © David S. Addison/Visuals Unlimited; p. 19 (inset), © Dennis Green/Survival Anglia; pp. 20-21, © Gerald
Cubitt/Bruce Coleman Limited; pp. 22-23, Pat Ortega, 1992; p. 24, © Pat Ortega, 1992

Cover photograph, © Jeff Foott/Bruce Coleman Limited: A jaguar rests on the rain forest floor in Belize. The jaguar
is losing its forest home in much of Central and South America to loggers cutting lumber to sell and to clear land
for farming.

Series editor: Elizabeth Kaplan
Editor: Valerie Weber
Series designer: Sabine Beaupré
Picture researcher: Diane Laska

Printed in MEXICO

3 4 5 6 7 8 9 98 97 96

Contents

Exploring Our Environment 4
Life and Death on Earth..............................7
Sad Times for Animals 8
Hunting to Death 10
Illegal Trade 12
Killing Animals to Protect Livestock? 15
No Room for Animals 17
Hidden Destroyers 19
How Can You Help?.................................20
Extinction Is Forever 22

More Books to Read 23
Places to Write 23
Glossary 23
Index 24

Words printed in **boldface** type the first time they occur in the text
appear in the glossary.

Exploring Our Environment

Look around you. You see forests, fields, rivers, and oceans. You see plants, animals, trees, and birds. All of these things make up our **environment**. We share the environment with all the other living things on Earth. But we often cause problems for the creatures with which we share the environment. For example, because of our actions, many different kinds of animals are dying out. Why is this happening? Let's find out.

4

Life and Death on Earth

The Earth is more than 4.5 billion years old.
The first living thing appeared about 3.5
billion years ago. Since then, many types of
plants and animals have **evolved**.

As new **species** of animals evolved, older
species died out, or became **extinct**. Animals
become extinct when they can't **adapt** to
changes in their environment. For example,
the dinosaurs became extinct 65 million years
ago. Since life began on Earth, thousands of
species of animals have disappeared.

Sad Times for Animals

Extinction is a natural process. But in the past 400 years, animal species have been dying out faster than ever before. This is because people have changed the Earth so much that many types of animals can no longer survive.

Animals at risk for becoming extinct are known as **endangered species**. More than 700 types of animals are endangered. All the animals shown on these two pages are endangered. The following pages describe some of our actions that endanger animals all over the world.

Hunting to Death

People have always hunted animals for food or fur. But sometimes we hunt down too many of one kind of animal. Then the animal becomes endangered.

10

Overhunting has endangered many types of whales and fur seals. Giant tortoises, native to isolated islands around the world, were once a source of meat for sailors. Overhunting has reduced their numbers so that now all are either endangered or extinct.

11

Illegal Trade

Some animals are endangered because people trap too many of them. They sell the animals to scientific researchers, animal collectors, or zoos. Many of the animals are not cared for correctly before they're sold. Some die from overcrowding. Some die from disease. Some die because they're fed the wrong foods. Some die simply from being pent up in a small cage for weeks at a time. Although it is illegal to trap and sell many types of rare animals, the wildlife trade continues.

12

Killing Animals to Protect Livestock?

People believe that certain animals pose a danger to humans or farm animals. Cheetahs sometimes chase down stray cattle. Wolves and grizzly bears may prey on sheep. Bald eagles at times attack chickens. But none of these animals regularly goes after farm animals. Most hunt other wild animals. Still, the stories of killer animals remain. Cheetahs, wolves, grizzly bears, and bald eagles are all endangered because people have poisoned, trapped, or hunted them, mistakenly thinking this will protect their livestock.

No Room for Animals

But the main reason that many animals are endangered is because people are destroying their **habitats**, the places where animals live. We chop down forests for farms. We drain swamps to build houses. We dam fast-flowing rivers to provide electricity. We pave huge areas to build cities.

All of these actions drive animals away. They can no longer find food, shelter, or safe places to raise families. Unable to adapt, they die out.

17

Hidden Destroyers

Some of the ways we have destroyed animals' habitats aren't so obvious. For example, when Europeans first came to Australia, they brought rats, foxes, and cats. The new animals preyed upon the native animals. Soon hundreds of Australian species disappeared.

Pollution also causes problems. Fish die off when lakes and rivers become polluted. Pollution from **pesticides** makes the eggshells of peregrine falcons and other birds of prey weak and brittle. The baby birds die before they can hatch.

How Can You Help?

Many organizations are working to help endangered animals. Some groups convince governments to make laws to prevent poachers, like the ones shown here, from killing endangered animals and selling their skins, furs, or feathers. Zookeepers try to learn about endangered animals and **breed** them. Then they can return the young animals to their homes in the wild. You can help animals that are at risk by joining any of the organizations that work to protect our many endangered animals.

20

Extinction Is Forever

Once an animal becomes extinct, it is gone forever. Nothing we can do will bring back the animals shown here: the colorful Carolina parakeet, the white wolf of eastern Canada, the Portuguese ibex. Each of these animals became extinct about 100 years ago, killed off by human hunters. But endangered animals do not have to disappear. By protecting them and the places where they live, we make the world a richer, more varied place.

More Books to Read

Mountain Gorillas in Danger by Rita Ritchie (Gareth Stevens)
Close to Extinction by John Burton (Watts)
Why Are Whales Vanishing? by Isaac Asimov (Gareth Stevens)

Places to Write

Here are some places you can write to for more information about endangered animals. Be sure to tell them exactly what you want to know about. Give them your full name and address so they can write back to you.

Environmental Defense Fund
   National Headquarters
257 Park Avenue South
New York, New York 10010

National Audubon Society
950 Third Avenue
New York, New York 10022

Wildlife Information Center, Inc.
629 Green Street
Allentown, Pennsylvania 18102

World Wildlife Fund
90 Eglinton Avenue East
Suite 504
Toronto, Ontario M4P 2Z7

Glossary

adapt (uh-DAPT): to become adjusted to something; animals adapt to changes in their environment or become extinct.

breed: to mate and give birth to offspring, or young.

endangered species: types of animals that are in danger of dying out or becoming extinct.

environment (en-VIE-run-ment): the natural and artificial things that make up the Earth.

23

evolve (ee-VAWLV): to develop gradually from something else; complex animals evolved from simpler animals.

extinct (eks-TINKT): when a type of animal, plant, or other organism dies out.

habitat (HAB-ih-tat): the type of environment in which a specific kind of animal or plant normally lives.

pesticide (PEHS-tih-side): a chemical put on plants to kill insects that eat or cause disease in the plant.

species (SPEE-sheez): a group of animals or plants that are considered to be all of the same type; animals that are in danger of dying out are called endangered species.

Index

Australia 18

bald eagles 15

Carolina parakeet 22
cheetahs 15

dinosaurs 7

endangered species 9
evolution 7
extinction 9, 11, 22

fur seals 11

grizzly bears 15

habitat destruction 17
hunting 22

overhunting 11

peregrine falcons 18
pesticides 18

pollution 18
Portuguese ibex 22

tortoises, giant 11

whales 11
wildlife trade 12
wolves 15, 22

zoos 12